I0472692

How To Invest In Startups

CONTENTS

INTRODUCTION

A startup is an entrepreneurial project, usually started by a small group of individuals or a single person. Startups are "gazelle companies": growing young ventures that are built to create wealth. They are smart, innovative and fresh. These firms mostly offer an innovative product or service to consumers. Startups begin like a seed in someone's mind. It grows into an idea that can be executed to produce revenues, profits and employment numbers depending on the individuals and industry involved.

Startups differ from conventional businesses and small to medium-sized enterprises (SMEs) that do not promote innovative products and services. Startups also vary greatly from other business models that exist primarily to secure the livelihood of the founders without any substantial growth perspective.

Startups are important economic drivers that create wealth by adding new products or services to the market, creating a significant number of jobs. Today, startups area flooding the entire marketplace and turning the average Joes into moneymaking venture capitalists.

Venture capital (VC) is a pretty basic concept. An entrepreneur has a brilliant idea, does the research to create a credible and full picture of the available market, and presents it to private investors who are expert at assessing opportunities. The investor, if convinced of the idea and confident of the proposed management team may decide to go ahead and negotiate an aggressive return on their investment in return for taking on the financial risk. That is basically what a venture capitalist does—providing venture capital to make a return on their investment.

While it's true that many great companies turn to traditional venture capital —with little or no individual access—for funding, startups are opening up to the idea of other alternatives. With certain models, you can create a deal flow of bona fide "VC-grade" investment opportunities and play at the same level, and on the same terms, as the big firms.

This means that you don't have to go to your uncles'-neighbours'-kids'-guitar-teachers' startup if you want to get skin in the VC game. Alone, building serious deal flow can take a lot of work, but exceptional companies are now becoming available to individuals through reputable vehicles. The best part? They're usually accessible for a reasonable minimum.

Exorbitant fees, carry and minimum investment are usually what turn off newer investors. The idea of investing hundreds of thousands of pounds in a very risky asset-class is not for the faint-hearted (or risk-averse). While it's true that "It takes money to make money" applies to venture capital, there are investment vehicles that will not only charge reasonable fees and carry, but encourage a more diversified and manageable portfolio via smaller contributions.

Hundreds of thousands of businesses are formed every year. Many of them are in significant need of capital, presenting opportunities for investors. And today, startup investors are hitting the goldmine—making 20 to 50 times their investments with diverse portfolios.

While startup investing is not for everyone, those with a high risk tolerance can find it a stimulating and potentially rewarding pastime. The possibility of getting in on the ground floor of the next Uber or Facebook, speculative as that might be, can be compelling.

NINE REASONS TO INVEST IN A STARTUP

1. It helps build a better world. Innovative startups are building a better place for all of us, and your investments will enable them to do so. Many of those who will change our lives for the better are still in a garage with that idea that'd would revolutionise everything.

2. It is now easy to reduce risks. There are networks that enable you to easily build portfolios of great startups, that have been thoroughly screened by investors like you — some of them who know in and out the industry where each startup operates.

3. It is a great way to diversify your investment. Whether in good or bad times, the startup community creates value. These are medium to long term investments that have low correlation with other assets classes.

4. It is an enriching experience. More and more investors are building portfolios and obtaining nicely positive returns. With most of them getting 20 to 50 times their investments!

5. It helps you build a network of like-minded people. Exchanging your views with other potential investors on the startups that present to you is a great way to connect with new people.

6. It keeps you young and boosts your morale. It keeps you up to date with the latest innovations, giving you a first-hand taste of what the future holds for business industries.

7. You can do good while doing well.

You can invest in startups that sustain the values that you believe in — and do well by doing so.

8. You can contribute to the success of the startups you invest in.
Entrepreneurs also take investment as a way to build a network of people which will help them, and often welcome help and expertise. You can leverage your network and expertise, whether on product, recruitment, access to the market, new investors or accessing potential company buyers.

9. You provide employment. Startups are great job-creating tools. Getting involved in startups puts you in a place to support this tried and true method of job creation, once again producing positive externalities to benefit the countries your startups operate in as you diversify your personal portfolio.

STARTING OUT: ANALYSING YOUR FIRST INVESTMENT

Thinking about investing in a startup? Suppose you hear about an exciting new company looking for investors. You are aware that a majority of startups end up failing within the first few years, but you think this one could hit it big. What do you do?

A lot of people are attracted to startup investing—who wouldn't want to be an early investor in companies like AirBnB, Spotify or Google?

However, the process can still be overwhelming to many. How do I start investing in startups? How much can I invest? Where do I find a startup to invest in? How do I select the right startup for my investment?

THE PROBLEM

The first thing you should understand about a startup is the problem they are trying to solve. Some problems might seem minor, but even a small problem that is a problem to a lot of people can be significant.

Innovative ideas are often associated with startups. However, an innovative idea might not be a solution to any significant problems. More important than building ideas, is solving problems that matter.

The first thing to understand in a startup is, "What problem are they trying to solve?" This is an important question to ask when considering to invest in a startup. Ask yourself, is this something that needs to be solved? Is this company making something that I want to exist in the world? Are there other people who need this? Is it a big enough problem that someone would be willing to pay for it to be solved?

People are constantly looking for new ways to solve their problems. As long as they have problems, they will be searching for easier, faster, cheaper, and smarter ways to improve their everyday life. Hence, a company that can offer a solution to a burning problem, will have a head start because they already have potential customers with a need for the offered solution.

Be clear to differentiate between a 'must have' and a 'nice to have' solution. A 'must have' product or service offers a solution to an urgent and important problem, while a 'nice to have' product or service is solving a problem, that is neither urgent nor important. In some cases, the people might not even recognize they have a problem.

What Problem Is The Startup Trying To Solve?

To figure out what problem the startup is trying to solve, it is important to understand the different perceptions of problems. Some problems might seem minor, but even a small problem, that is a problem to a lot of people, can be significant. When a problem is significant for enough people, there will be a demand for a solution to it.

A market, where many people have big problems, seemingly has huge potential, but keep in mind that such markets most likely already have many competitors present. Differentiation becomes the key here.

Potential also lies in small problems that many people have. Let's take Airbnb as an example. Two groups of people had a small problem. Travellers, who didn't have enough money to stay in hotels or had a tough time finding accommodation, and apartment owners, who wanted some additional revenue. Airbnb spotted this problem and solved it.

The opposite is also worth noting, some problems are important but only for a small number of people. Let's use designers as an example. They were lacking a design and prototyping tool, that focused on collaboration and sharing their designs with others. Here's where InVision came to the rescue.

These problems are harder to identify because people, who are not working in the design field, will probably not have this problem. Therefore, it is harder to recognize problems outside of our own fields, that we are not involved in.

It is important to see the bigger picture and understand how big of a problem the startup is actually planning to solve. To understand what problem the startup is solving and whether it is a significant one, it is necessary to do as much research as possible.

Ask yourself, does the startup solve a big enough problem that someone is willing to pay for the solution?

Does It Matter To You?

Consider whether the company is doing something which matters to you personally. If the company is working within an industry you understand, there's a bigger chance that you will be able to contribute to the success of the company, both directly as a client, by giving the company advice, mentorship, or introductions; and by shouting about the company to the relevant audience that is your network.

THE SOLUTION

Once you have pinned down the problem, look into how the startup is solving it. What is the product or service they are offering? After you have figured it out, it is important to find out, how that solution is different from others. Ask yourself, what makes their idea unique?

Another important thing to consider when looking into their solution is whether it creates a viable business model. Without one, the startup will have a tough time generating revenue and from an investor's point of view, it will not be a wise investment if the company won't become profitable.

Does It Solve The Problem And Can We Make Money Doing So?

First, it is important to look into how the startup is solving the problem. Once the problem is identified, it's time to look what solution the startup has come up with. A good start would be to map down their business idea.

Making sense of the solution the startup offers requires asking yourself the right questions, and figuring out the startup and its idea in more depth.

1. What is the solution that they're offering?

2. What is the idea they're presenting?

3. What is the product or service they're offering?

4. Are they even solving the problem?

Once the business idea or the solution is defined, it's important to ask, who are the people who need it. The key here is to look at the startup's value proposition. Value proposition focuses on how the company is creating value to its customers.

Why Is The Solution Unique?

Once you have figured out how the startup solves the problem, it is worth asking, what makes their solution unique. What are the key features that differentiate their product or service from others? Asking these questions help to understand the competitive advantage that makes them different from the competitors.

Startups, who have created a unique solution or have a competitive advantage over their competitors, have better odds to do well compared to startups who haven't.

One aspect that helps to determine the uniqueness of the solution is owning patents, proprietary solutions or other types of intellectual property. When a startup has one of those, it counts as a competitive advantage and the company is then protected from others copying that solution. This is definitely a good sign.

On the other side, not owning any patents or proprietary solutions, doesn't mean the startup is destined to fail. Often startups lack the funds, time or other means to file for patents, and find it more important to go to the market and start generating revenue.

Software solutions can be more difficult to patent since they need to meet specific patentability criteria. In those cases, the uniqueness of the solution can lie in better customer service, smarter marketing or better business effectiveness than the competitors'.

Does The Solution Create A Viable Business Model?

No matter how unique the solution is, it has to be possible to make money using it. This is where the business plan comes into play. The business model defines how the startup will generate revenue from its idea.

The idea that the startup is working with often determines their business model. It should be the heart of every startup because, without a clear plan to generate revenue, the company will struggle to make money and survive in the long run.

There is no universal business model that works for everyone. Different types of businesses require different types of business models. Determining if the business model the startup has chosen, is viable, needs to be looked at in a case-by-case manner.

THOROUGHLY RESEARCH THE STARTUP

Ask lots of questions and request lots of documents. If the business is concerned about revealing confidential information, it can have you sign a nondisclosure agreement. You and your advisors will want to examine the startup's business plan, offering memorandum, financial statements, budgets, capitalization table, and corporate documents (articles, bylaws, prior investor agreements, etc.) If the documents are shoddy or incomplete, that is a bad sign. Be wary of internal financial statements; statements prepared by an outside CPA have more credibility. Audited financial statements are best, but are less common because of their expense. If your investigation raises red flags, insist on complete explanations.

Review The Investment Documents

Your advisors can be of great help here. At the very least, you want to be fully informed as to how the deal is being structured and what rights and obligations you and the company will have. Your attorney can advise you as to what document changes might be in your best interests and help you negotiate with the company. Your accountant can let you know whether the valuation seems reasonable. Do not proceed unless everything is fully documented. You should not invest based on a handshake or mere verbal assurances.

Understand The Risks

Think thoroughly about your risk tolerance and consider the possible outcomes beforehand. Investors always risk losing all of the invested money when the startup ceases to exist. So unless you are willing to take such risk, don't invest in a startup. Only invest the money you can afford to lose. Even if the startup becomes successful, it can take years before you see any return on investment.

Aside from understanding the general risk when investing in startups, it's also important to understand the specific risks with the company you are analysing. Where are their weaknesses? Are those things you believe they can improve on? A good question to ask a company is: "If your company does not exist in 18 months, what would be the reason?"

This question is not intended to test the confidence of a founder or expose weakness; it's intended to understand the imagination of the founders, and their ability to anticipate risks to their business. If a founder says, that there are no risks, it means that they are overly confident, and this puts you more at risk. Look for reflected, humble answers, and reasonable courses of action that the founders can take to address them.

The deal (investment terms)

This part requires the most knowledge from you as an investor, and unless you are an experienced investor, you definitely need to seek professional advice or co-invest with someone who knows exactly what they are doing.

Ultimately, the deal you can get reflects the situation that the company is in. No company, especially with as early-stage as startups are, will be doing perfectly everywhere. A company that has little or no traction, will have to offer to sell equity at a lower valuation than a company that already has a lot of traction.

CROWDFUNDING

Crowdfunding has never been more revelant to start investing, with new online platforms popping up ever more frequently. And with equity crowdfunding, startup investing is finally available to everyone. Many consider it to be the future of investing, others warn that its risks are often underestimated. And then there are the different types of crowdfunding: reward-based, equity-based, debt-based, flexible, fixed and so on. It can all seem bewildering, but like most things the underlying logic is simple.

The most important benefit to crowdfunding is that it makes investment in small companies and startups accessible to everybody. For this reason, it is more important than ever for people to fully understand this new world, as most of the negative publicity around crowdfunding is largely focused on misuse and misunderstanding of the platforms.

WHAT IS THE CROWD?

Ordinary, everyday people. And that's what the 'crowd' in crowdfunding refers to. You see, raising money is not really about business plans or market traction or financial forecasts: it's ultimately about trust. And in life, the higher the risk of being hurt, the more important trust becomes. For this reason, most people don't mind putting a few pounds towards sponsoring a charity run or lending a friend a few pounds; there's a general acceptance that you shouldn't expect to see that money again, and as such the level of trust in the person to whom you are giving the money doesn't need to be particularly high.

But if somebody asks you to invest several thousand pounds, the situation is radically different. For most people, this is not an amount of money that they can afford to lose. Therefore, most people have been locked out of the investment world where small businesses need thousands of pounds to be invested.

It's therefore logical that the traditional routes for founders financing a business have been channels like loans from banks, high net worth individuals and friends and family. A founder's ability to raise money has depended largely on their collateral in the case of a bank loan, or their personal network in the case of investments from individuals, and consisted of big chunks of money from a small handful of people who trust them and/

or have thoroughly vetted them. The alternative—raising small chunks of money from a large number of people—has been largely impossible unless the founder happens to know hundreds of people and is both willing and able to deal with the enormous administrative overhead of dealing with so many people.

Enter the internet, with its well-established history of both removing administrative headaches and connecting large groups of people together. Crowdfunding essentially facilitates the matchmaking between ordinary people who are interested in investing in things and ordinary founders who don't happen to have access to collateral or large networks of wealthy individuals. The software running the crowdfunding platform handles all of the administration, while the internet itself provides a vast potential pool of people for the founder to market to, at scale.

In short, crowdfunding makes it possible to raise small amounts of money from a large amount of total strangers. For that reason, it's great.

EQUITY-BASED CROWDFUNDING

Equity crowdfunding is a form of investing that involves many individuals investing online in a business in return for share capital, whether through a dedicated equity crowdfunding platform or independently organized by the company itself.

In the past four years, more than 2,000 companies have raised about 175 million with zero cases of fraud in the U.K. In the last few years numerous equity crowdfunding platforms have come up in US such as Seedrs, CircleUp, Crowdfunder, and Fundable.

Much closer to the traditional notion of investing, equity-based platforms facilitate investments in businesses in exchange for equity in those businesses. Legit online equity platforms like are regulated by the Financial Conduct Authority in the UK and their investors must meet certain legal requirements.

These are, however, not particularly stringent and usually involve a simple credit check and completion of an online questionnaire. Minimum investment amounts are still very accessible at around the £10 mark usually, although some equity platforms have a higher minimum stake.

For businesses looking to raise, however, the entry process is much tougher. Proper legal due diligence is performed on every company, and the submission process normally consists of a number of rounds of iteration and approval before the campaign can go live. The obvious benefit for investors is the added layer of protection for their investment. It is much rarer for scammers or fraudsters to launch on equity platforms and FCA regulations require claims by the businesses to be backed up with evidence which the platform will verify themselves before allowing the campaign to launch. For this reason, as many as 90% of all applications for equity-based platforms fail to make it through to campaign launch.

The advantages for businesses raising money are access to a more sophisticated group of investors beyond their own networks (traditional investors are increasingly flocking to such platforms), as well as a streamlined process for dealing with the- generally much smaller than other crowdfunding platforms - group of investors. There is also an increasing trend for equity platforms acting as nominee shareholders on behalf of the investors, which means the business takes on a single new shareholder instead of several hundred, making administration much easier as well as making future investments far more straightforward.

Equity platforms will normally hold the funds in escrow until the campaign is over, adding yet another layer of protection for investors. Of course, the normal risks apply in terms of expected returns: most investments will not return much if anything, but the ones that do promise huge financial gains compared to other investment options. Generally speaking, this type of crowdfunding is what is referred to in speculations about the impact of the format on the future of investing generally.

Technology Trends Driving Equity Crowdfunding

Digital equity crowdfunding: Combining blockchain technology and equity crowdfunding, decentralized exchanges are being used to create digital stock offerings. The appeal of digital-based equity crowdfunding is that it is easier to create an aftermarket once a sale takes place as well as marketing the offering around the globe.

Smartphones are take crowdfunding mainstream. With 24/7 mobile access, investors are constantly exposed to new fundraising initiatives—from a political campaign, to a new tech gadget, or even a cross-border investment in a promising new start-up.

Investment clubs are moving online. Investment clubs are moving their operations online and social investing will take a giant leap forward. Investors will leverage personal connections to create online syndicates for start-up investments, forming not just social circles but rather new investment circles.

REGULATIONS IN THE U.S. AND EUROPE FOR EQUITY CROWDFUNDING

The U.K.: Crowdfunding in the European Union (EU) is regulated by the same sets of laws that govern financial institutions, notably lenders (e.g., banks) and investment entities (e.g., venture capital firms, and angel investors). The Prospectus European Directive specifies the information that has to be transmitted to investors for funding targets over €5 million.

Funding targets of less than €100,000 are exempted throughout the EU while national authorities are allowed to specify rules governing amounts between €100,000 and €5 million. Investment Services Directive (ISD) enables crowdfunding platforms to operate across all European countries using the so-called passport that enables any investment services firm regulated in one country to serve investors and issuers from other European countries.

The U.S.: The new rules and proposed amendments according to US Jobs Acts are designed to assist smaller companies with capital formation and provide investors with additional protections. Regulation crowdfunding permits individuals to invest in securities-based crowdfunding transactions subject to certain investment limits. The regulation allows a company to raise a maximum aggregate amount of $1 million through crowdfunding offerings in a period of 12 months.

The regulation in the U.S. enables individual investors, over a 12-month period, to invest in the following aggregate across all crowdfunding offerings: If either their annual income or net worth is less than $100,000, than the greater of:

If either their annual income or net worth is less than $100,000, than the greater of:

- $2,000 or

- 5 percent of the lesser of the annual income or net worth.

If both the annual income and the net worth are equal to or more than $100,000, 10 percent of the lesser of the annual income or net worth;

TAX RELIEF: SEIS AND EIS

WHAT IS SEIS?

Seed Enterprise Investment Scheme SEIS is a government approved scheme to encourage investment into early stage companies. It lowers an investor's risk of investing in young companies by them offering tax relief. Qualifying companies can raise up to £150,000 under the SEIS scheme.

An individual investor can invest as much £100,000 in any tax year. In return HMRC provides initial income tax relief of up to 50% of the value of the money invested. This automatically takes away 50% of the risk of investment.

If the company succeeds and the investors make a gain on the sale of his/her shares, the gain is exempt from Capital Gains Tax (CGT). If the company fails, the investors can offset the loss on the shares against their income tax bill.

This means there is a win-win on all sides. Investors have any potential risk reduced, Founders receive funding and the UK economy sees investment in its most innovative businesses.

WHAT IS EIS?

The Enterprise Investment Scheme (EIS) has been designed by the UK Government to encourage private investment into small, high-risk trading companies by offering a range of tax incentives.

For those companies which outgrow the SEIS scheme, the EIS scheme is available. It is SEIS's 'bigger sister', if you like and works in a similar way. Companies can raise up to £5,000,000 under the EIS scheme.

Any one individual investor can invest up to £1,000,000 per person per year in qualifying companies. Initial income tax relief is 30% of the value of the money invested. An added benefit is that EIS has a 'carry back' facility which allows for investments to be applied to the preceding tax year.

Did you know that:

1. SEIS and Enterprise Investment Scheme are designed to encourage investors to back early stage businesses. These incentives are very generous

and in some cases investors can be risking as little as £2k in a £10k startup investment.

2. HMRC underwrites up to 72.5% of the invested sums through income tax reliefs for investors and up to 100% of the investment could be underwritten with capital gain reliefs.

3. If the right conditions are met, there will be no tax to pay at exit.

FIVE WAY INVESTORS CAN OBTAIN SEIS / EIS TAX RELIEF

1. Initial investment. Income Tax relief is 50% (SEIS) or 30% (EIS) on the amount invested up to a maximum of £100k for SEIS and £1m for EIS per individual in a tax year. Example:

• If you invest £100k then under SEIS, you save £50k on your income tax or £30k under EIS.

• You claim the income tax relief for the tax year in which the shares were issued, or you can carry back the relief.

• Relief is limited to the extent there is an income tax liability to claim against.

2. Exit. The big one! No CGT to pay if shares are sold more than 3 years after investment. Example:

• If you invests £100k in a company and sells the shares 4 years later for £1m, then the £900k gain is tax free.

• This allows for a significant CGT saving of £180k!

3. Bust. If the worst happens and the company does not make it, an investor loses money. The loss on the shares disposed of can be set against the investor's income or capital gains to reduce his/her tax liability. This is important for limiting losses on the investment. Example:

• If an investor invests £100k into a startup. If the business is wound up, then the investor can obtain £22.5k (SEIS) or £31.5k (EIS) income tax relief on their loss, assuming they are a 45% tax rate payer.

- Their total loss is therefore £27.5k (27.5%) under SEIS or £38.5k (38.5%)under EIS including the income tax relief claimed after investment.

4. Initial investment — carry back. Amount subscribed for shares in SEIS/ EIS companies can be treated as if it was made in the tax year before the investment was made. Example:

- If no prior year SEIS investments were made, an investor can invest up to £200k (max £100k per company) with a saving of £100k (£200k at 50%) on their tax bill.

5. Initial investment — Loss relief against income on gains. Investors can claim an exemption for 50% of a capital gain realised in a tax year when the proceeds are re-invested in the same tax year in qualifying SEIS / EIS companies. This will save an investor 10% tax in the case of SEIS (i.e. 50% of the current CGT rate of 20%). Example:

- When an investor, with a capital gain of £100k which is taxable at 20%, makes a £100k investment into a qualifying SEIS company, the investor will save £10k in CGT (20% x 50% x £100k = £10k).

TAX RELIEF FROM INHERITANCE TAX

An investment in an SEIS or EIS qualifying company should qualify for 100% relief from Inheritance Tax, so long as the investment has been held for two years and is still held at time of death.

CAREFUL CONSIDERATION

EIS and SEIS are essentially "locked-in" products. You need to be able to leave the investments locked in for a period of at least three years (and in some cases longer) in order to access the tax relief benefits—managers will generally look for an exit in or around year four, but an exit could realistically take longer and is subject to market conditions. In this way, many EIS and SEIS companies are illiquid and the secondary market for selling EIS/SEIS shares is therefore small.

RETURNS AFTER INVESTMENT

Startups investment offer various types of returns dependent on the company's performance and its potential to exit.

There are many ways to exit the business, some positive and success-driven, others negative and failure-driven. Sometimes companies also pay dividends, another immediate form of return on investment.

Having an exit strategy is especially important when investing in startups. Investing in one can tie up your funds for some time, depending on the business of course. Unlike companies, who are on the stock market, startup shares cannot be sold as quickly and easily. As an investor, it is, therefore, important for you to lay out a plan of how to sell off your stake.

There are basically two ways for a company to exit: Acquisition or entering the stock market. In the first case, the company gets acquired by another one and you as an investor will be able to exit and possibly profit from the investment. The other option is an IPO, Initial Public Offering, at which point the investor may choose to sell their shares or keep them as stocks.

Of all parts of the investment process, the exit strategy is undeniably the favourite of angel investors and entrepreneurs. The exit strategy is when a venture capitalist or entrepreneur intends to cash in on an investment.

There are different forms of exit strategies that investors and entrepreneurs to plan out in order to get that return of investment:

1. Initial Public Offer. For startup businesses, an exit strategy could be the Initial Public Offer (IPO) wherein a part of the business is sold to the public in the form of shares. This way, entrepreneurs are reimbursing investors within their own startup. Aside from that, the business gets more access to liquidity for investors and more chances to acquire other companies.

2. Mergers and Acquisitions. Startups can do well with exercising the option to merge with another company if problems with cash flow or liquidity arise. With mergers and acquisitions, the new business stays afloat and provides security among investors.

3. Private Offerings. Another exit strategy is to conduct a private offering of the business' shares to individuals or a select group of investors to raise funds, which is more cost effective because brokers are not required. This can be done with crowd funding websites and real estate. The private offering is not registered with Companies House, and are exempt from required reporting arrangements and allows for existing shareholders to be bought out in a new fundraiser round.

4. Cash Cow. Cash cows are firms that can command a high market share in an industry dominated by low growth. They are able to sustain enough capital to stay afloat and have increased profits over the years to pay dividends to investors and shareholders by cashing in on their products.

5. Regulation A+. Regulation A+ is similar to IPO. The business owner can put your startup company on an exchange after qualifying. The entrepreneur can benefit from raising money and conforming to particular stipulations laid down by the Companies House without having to publish accounts publicly or file other mandatory paper works that would be required of an IPO.

6. Venture Capital. A good way to secure investors is to keep the cash rolling into the startup. Often, a venture capitalist would invest large sums of money into businesses and startups that are deemed worthy of note. Although this takes time for the investment to mature, it is able to provide a steady source of cash to create more investments, expand development, and attract other wealthy investors who see the potential for high returns in the future. More real estate crowdfunding companies are going into venture capital.

It's worth noting, that some companies might not have an exit strategy, but can give returns to investors in other ways.

THE CHECKLIST

To sum this all up, I have prepared a checklist. The more "yes" answers you get, the better. But keep in mind, that a startup does not have to check out on every question. If they would, then they probably wouldn't be asking you for an investment.

1. Market. For a company to become successful, there needs to be a market for the products or services they are offering. Even though the solution sounds great, if there is no market for it, it will not generate revenue and therefore not give you the expected return on investment.

To understand the market, it needs to be analysed. Who is going to buy this product? How many people have this need that has to be solved? Is the market big enough? Or is it more of a niche market? What is the target market of the startup? Is it an existing, emerging, or new market?

A startup must also have a go-to-market or a marketing strategy. Without one, no matter how great the target market and their solution sounds, they will have a tough time getting to the market to start generating revenue.

2. Monetised. This may seem like an obvious tip but you'd be shocked how many investors get hyped up over the novelty of an idea and lose focus on whether it can actually make money. Many high-concept businesses sound great on paper, but not in practice. Look carefully at the main source of revenue, the company's structure, and determine whether it is viable.

Lots of companies are based on an intriguing concept. But the company must be able to translate that concept into a product or service that it can produce and sell at a profit and in sufficient quantities to generate reasonable cash flow. What is the startup's monetization plan? What is the market demand? Who are the competitors? What is the marketing strategy? Is the business scalable, having the ability to grow rapidly without sacrificing quality or profitability? If the company is unable to provide good answers to these questions, its likelihood of success is dubious.

3. Analyse their competitors. Competition is always something to have an eye out for as a business but also as an investor. Get to know the competitors in their market, learn their advantages and disadvantages. It will give a nice overview of the competitive landscape of that market.

Every startup thinks they're a unicorn and that their new idea is going to revolutionise the industry. But there are literally thousands of start-ups popping up every day and there is bound to be an overlap of ideas — as the saying goes, there's nothing new under the sun.

Conducting your own due diligence is crucial before you make any investment decision

Venturing into a new idea or industry is extremely risky if you don't thoroughly analyse the players in the market. Find out current, past and future potential competitors, direct and indirect. Make sure the business idea you're backing has a unique intellectual property or operates in an industry with high barriers to entry, so it doesn't burn out too soon.

Use this overview to assess the startup's competitive advantage. What makes them different? What do they have that the competitors don't? How do they stack up against their competitors regarding other aspects like price, features, performance, etc.?

4. Team. Most companies will say that their team is the most important thing, and usually, it is. A good team early on is a crucial factor in running a successful startup. With the right people behind a good idea, the company can quickly find the right path and become profitable.

But how do you know, if the people running the startup are the right ones? The team members' background stories are the key here. What is their previous experience? What are they specialized in? What is their education? Have they run a business before and if so, how did it go? This should give a general overview of what value the team brings to the company.

You ultimately are investing not just in a product or an idea, but in the people running the company. No matter how innovative or promising the business concept may seem, the enterprise is unlikely to succeed without capable management. You should assess not only the founders, but also those promoting the investment. An initial review often can be done online. You want the people running or associated with the company to not only have clean backgrounds, but also a record of success in other ventures. Look for qualities such as experience, intelligence, creativity, integrity, discipline, and leadership ability.

Another good tip for evaluating a team is to remember, that at the end of the day, any company is just a collection of people, so ask yourself: "Is this a group of people who can accomplish something great together?" Running a startup is super tough, and if the team won't work well under pressure, this provides a great risk for you as an investor.

5. Traction. Having traction means that the startup already has some evidence of market adoption. This is an indicator to the investor, that there is a real need out there and people are getting interested in the products or services provided. It is definitely a good sign when a startup can provide some data supporting their claims. It shows that the team is committed to move things forward and make things happen.

Some key indicators that measure the traction of a startup can be the number of users/clients, revenue, cost per acquisition and customer lifetime value, engagement and website traffic, etc. Regardless, it all comes down to the startup you want to invest in and what type of business they run. Therefore the traction indicators can vary slightly.

The traction of the company is closely related to your risk tolerance, which we'll get more into in a later post. In general, the earlier stage the company —and the less traction it has—the higher the risk of the startup's failure. However, less traction also means lower valuation.

6. Use of funds. As an investor, you probably want to know how the startup will use your investment. Usually, startups need investments to fund their growth but this is such a broad reason. Therefore it is wise to dig deeper and figure out what are the exact goals of the startup and how do they plan to achieve them with the help of the investment.

A good idea is to look for the milestones set by the company. How do they plan to achieve them? How are they allocating the funds to reach those milestones? Is the investment reasonable for fulfilling the goals? What exactly will they achieve with the funds raised?

THE RISK FACTOR

Investing in startups is riskier than investing in the stock markets. However, the potential returns are huge compared to the ones you can get investing in stocks. Imaging if you could have bought shares of Tesla or Netflix before they went public, you would have multiplied your investment at least 20 times. Also, the tax incentives in some countries make this type of investment more attractive, and now, available to anyone thanks to the internet.

Not everyone has the same risk tolerance level, some people don't like risk at all, others are risk takers. Regardless of where you are, the reality is that no one likes losing money. Statistics show that 9 out of 10 startups will fail, but even with that, many people still invest. Why? Because if you can make profit on one, that will cover your loses and make you profit. It's very important, especially when it comes to invest in startups, to have a very diversified portfolio. Apply the phrase "Don't put all your eggs in one basket" to your investment strategy.

CONCLUSION

Although the concept of startups has often been used in the field of the digital economy (which accounts for a major share of startups), there are many startups from other industries, like medicine, biotech and finance.

Ditching the millennial business theories and 'trendifying' business setups, the modern world startups have brought a fresh edge and positive vibe in the business world. The investor invests directly into the company, which in return issues new shares. The investor holds a direct equity interest in the operating company subject to the rights and risks of any other minority investor.

In the fast-paced economies facing a plethora of changes and cut- throat competition, startups have paved their way to survive, strive and succeed in the dynamic and ever-growing business world.

Until now, when businesses were interested in seeking investment pounds, they'd immediately think of accredited investors. With startup investing, there are no accreditation requirements for investors. That means anyone from an angel investor to the bag boy at the grocery store can buy a stake in businesses on these sites. This means entrepreneurs can reach out to friends and colleagues or attend crowdfunding events to put in money alongside the investors who see a business as a wise investment. Once a profile has been set up on one of these sites, business owners then have a place to direct people who ask about investing in their efforts, in addition to the strangers who will see it.

When looking for an investment opportunity that won't bleed you dry with high admin costs, try to invest alongside someone who invests their own money and makes money on the upside—this keeps everyone's interests aligned.

In conclusion, any investor will want the assurance that they will get their money back. Startup businesses need to have an exit strategy to motivate investors to cash in on their investments.